The Best Me

Mr. Mault's Class

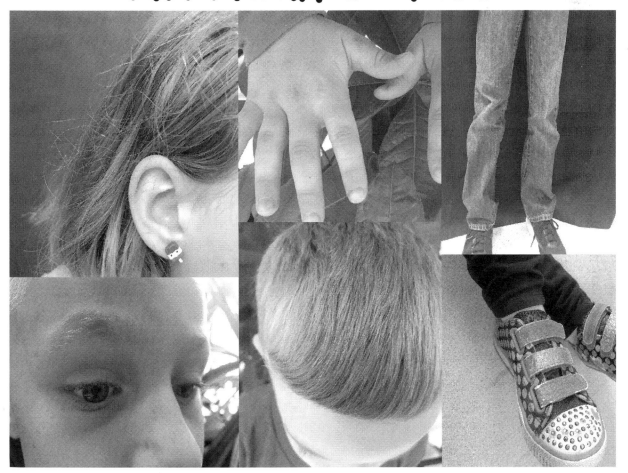

We are all unique. That is what makes us special. That is what makes our class, our country, and our world special. We may have only picked one part to describe in this book, but in reality, every single part of you is special and amazing.

The best part of you is YOU!
Keep being YOU!
YOU can move mountains.
YOU can change the world.
YOU are unstoppable.

YOU are amazing!

The Best Part of Me

By Mr. Mault's Class
2018-2019
Third Grade
Roy-Hart Elementary

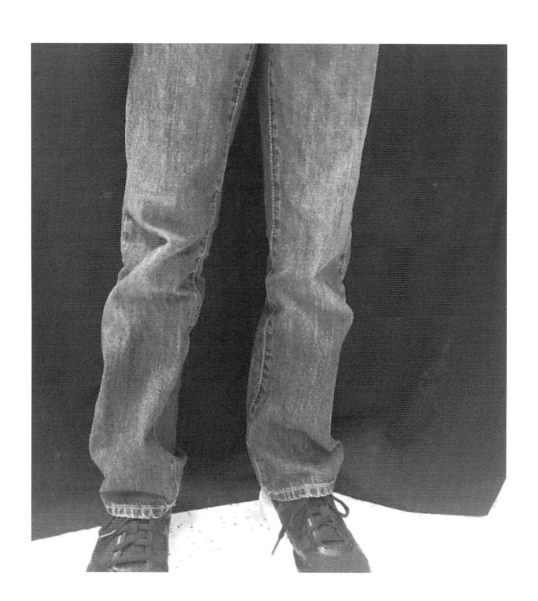

Legs

I like my legs because they help me play my favorite position which is midfield.
With my legs I can play soccer with my friends and soccer team.
If I didn't have my legs I couldn't walk or run or speed walk.
These are the reasons I think my legs or the best.

By: Declan

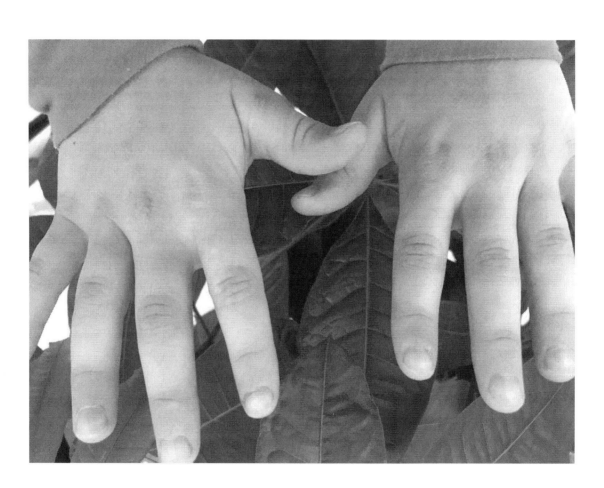

Hands

The best part of me is my hands.
I like my hands because they help me
write. I love to write about animals and
people. With my hands I can take care of
my cows I can feed them hay and grain. I
can groom them. If I didn't have my hands
I couldn't play the viola. I love to play the
viola.

These are the reasons I think my hands
are the best.

By: Lauren

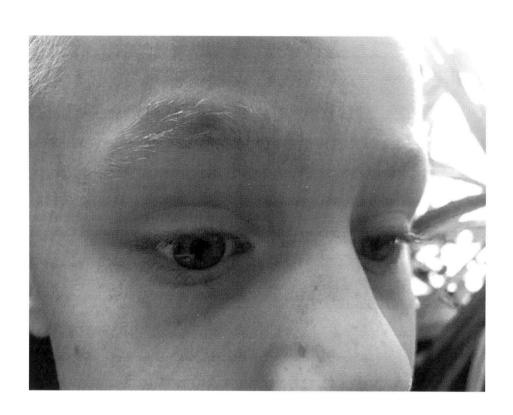

Eyes

The best part of me is my eyes I like my eyes because you can see. I can see my pets and my family with my eyes . With my eyes I can sports. I can see the bench the players and the puck. If I didn't have my eyes I could not play sports because I couldn't see things. I would run into people.

These are the reasons I think my eyes are the best.

By: Lincoln

Hands

I like my hands because I can hike the football. With my hands I can hold things I need. If I didn't have my hands I would not be able to to eat food or drink.

These are the reasons I think my hands are the best.

By: Jeffrey

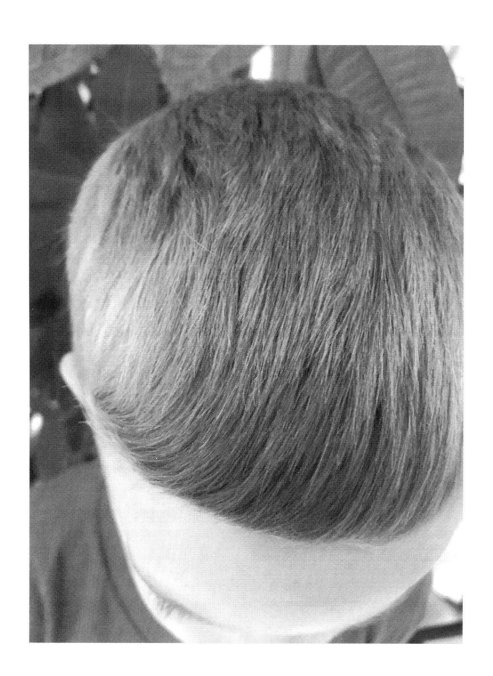

Hair

I like my hair because when it's a bit long it's really thick so I can play with it like jello. With my hair I can style it in a mohawk or just put it to the side. If I didn't have my hair I would be bald, ugly and look weird.

These are the reasons I think my hair is the BEST!!!

By: Benjamin

Feet

Feet, Feet you are the best. You help me walk and get out of bed. Without my feet I could not play
soccer or get on the bus.

I love you feet you feet. You are the best!

By: Autumn

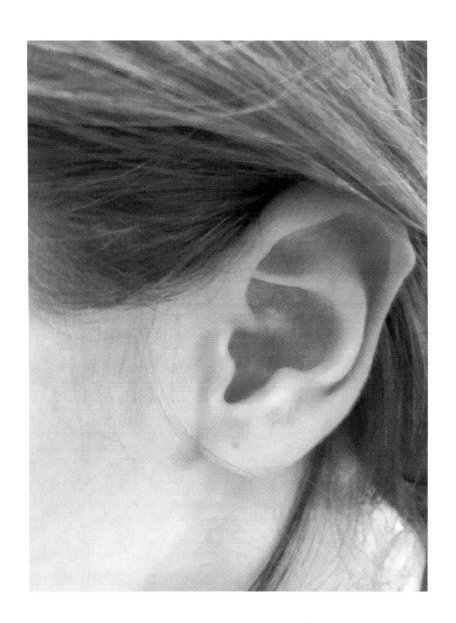

Ears

I like my ears because they help me listen to music. My favorite song is "I'm so Fancy." With my ears I can listen to teachers and parents and friends when there is an emergency. If I didn't have my ears I would not be able to listen to music and listen to reading and wear earrings.

These are the reasons I think my ears are the best.

By: Ruthie

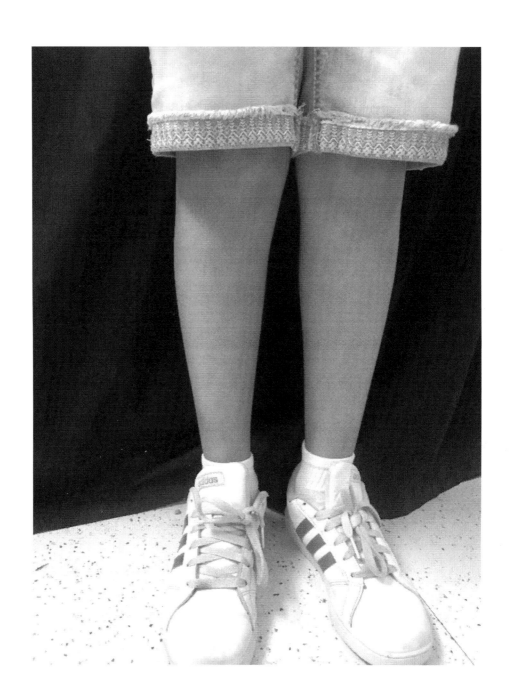

Legs

The best part of me is my legs. I like my legs because I couldn't do anything without my legs. I love my legs because they help me play soccer and my favorite position is center offense. With my legs I can play soccer, play catch, go on the playground and go on rides at Disney World. If I didn't have my legs I couldn't go to my cello practices or concerts and I couldn't even pick up my cello and that would be sad.

These are the reasons I think my legs are the best.

By: Sofia

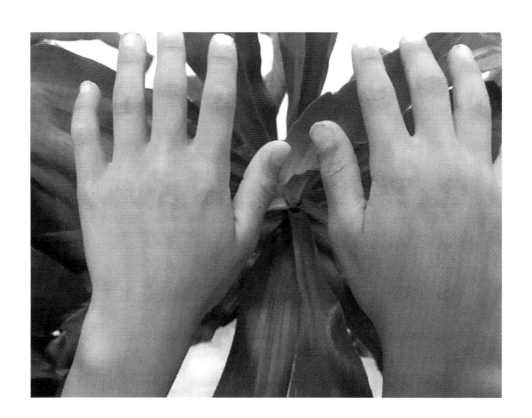

Hands

The best part of me are my hands. I like my hands because they help me read books. When I read books I build new neurons. With my hands I can play with my toys. My favorite toys are my tractors. If I didn't have my hands I wouldn't be able to do a lot of the stuff I do now. That would not be good.

These are the reasons I think my hands are the best.

By: Lucaiah

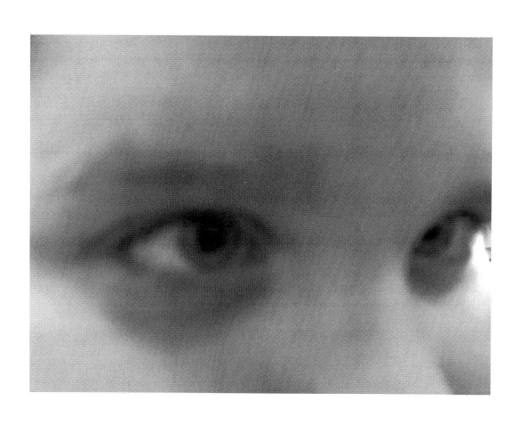

Eyes

The best me is my eyes. I like my eyes because I can watch the Yankees win the World Series again. With my eyes I can look for the football when my dad and I play catch. If I didn't have my eyes I couldn't read Captain Underpants or Diary of a Wimpy Kid.

These are the the reasons my eyes are the best.

By: John

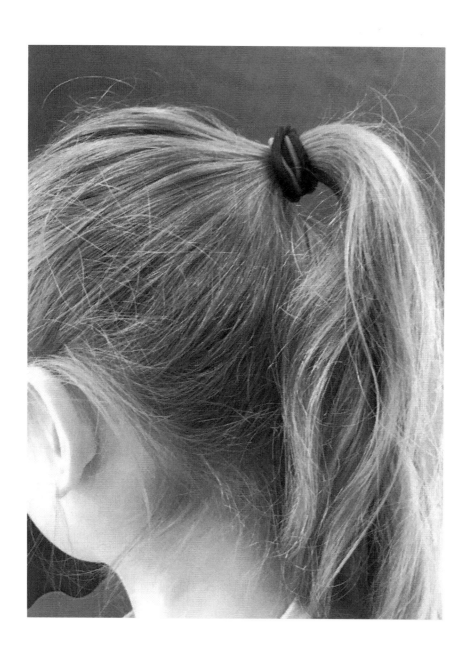

Hair

The best part of me is my hair. I like my hair because it is long and pretty and I can put pretty flowers in it! With my hair I can put it in a nice ponytail and in a nice french braid. If I didn't have my hair I might get made fun of a lot of times.

These are the reasons I think my hair is the best.

By: Addyson

Hands

The best part of me are my hands. I like my hands because hands can do a lot of things, like make a cake and open a door. With my hands I can pick up my dogs, cats,bunnies, polish chicken and turkeys. I can play the violin and take care of our horses. If I didn't have my have my hands I would not be able to do a lot of things.

These are the reasons I think my hands are the best.

By: Emma

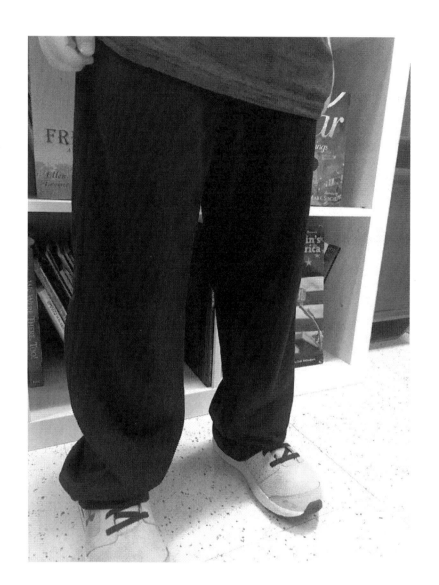

Legs

The best part of me is my legs. I love to run around and break wood. I love to jump kick things. With my legs I can play football and run and shin kick everyone. Well, only if I do not have shoes on. If I did not have my legs I could not do anything, because I could not move. I could not eat my favorite foods.

These are the reasons I think my legs are the best part of me.

By: Brody

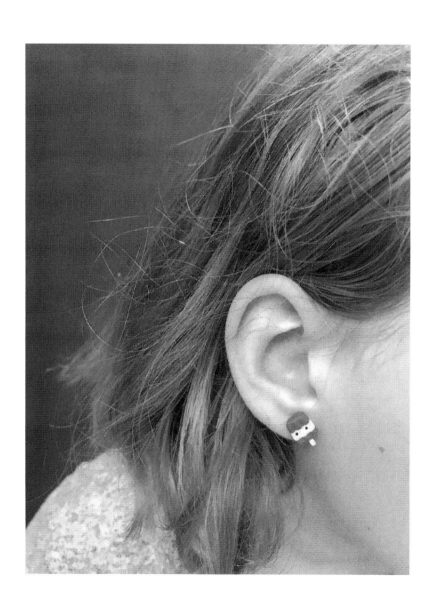

Ears

I like my ears because they hold the beautiful earrings I wear every single day. With my ears I can listen to beautiful piano music and music that makes you want to get up and dance. If I didn't have my ears I couldn't listen to piano music. I couldn't listen to stories when they are being read to me and my brother.

These are the reasons I think my ears are the best.

By: Ava

Hair

The best part of me is my hair.
I like my hair because it is long and it
keeps me warm in the winter. With my hair
I can put it in a long ponytail.
If I didn't have my hair, I would go crazy.
My hair makes me who I am.

Those are the reasons I think my hair is
the best.

By: Jade

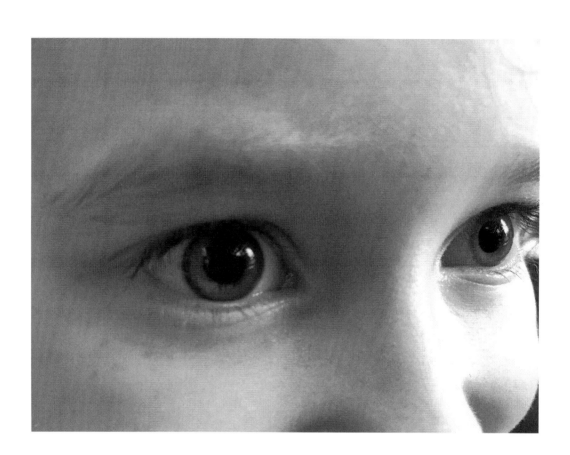

Eyes

The best part of me are my eyes. I like my eyes because I can see things that I want like a BFF or a book. With my eyes I can do well on a test or so you can see I you am going. If I didn't have my eyes I could not see anything. That would be bad. I would not be able to see tulips, which is my favorite flower.

These are the reasons I think my eyes are the best.

By: Cassidy

Hands

The best part of me are my hands. I like
my hands because I can hold
my pencil and write things. With my hands
I can wash my dads car when it's dirty.
If I didn't have my hands I wouldn't be
able to play baseball or golf.

These are the reasons I think my hands
are the best.

By: Tristan

Made in the USA
Monee, IL
19 August 2021